Therefore my heart is glad . . .
Psalm 16:9

Woman of God
Joy in the Journey

25 Devotions

Sue Logan ✶ Alison Zeller ✶ Carol Albrecht,
Kristin Schultz ✶ Pat Mitchell

CTA

The mission of CTA
is to glorify God by providing purposeful products
that lift up and encourage the body of Christ —
because we love him.

www.CTAinc.com

Sue Logan, Alison Zeller, Carol Albrecht,
Kristin Schultz, Pat Mitchell

Copyright © 2015 CTA, Inc.
1625 Larkin Williams Rd.
Fenton, MO 63026

PRINTED IN THAILAND
ISBN: 978-1-940088-29-7

Sarah
A Joyful Journey of Faith

Sarah is portrayed in the Bible's book of Hebrews as a woman of God, not because of what she accomplished, but because of what God accomplished through her. Sarah struggled and failed, just like you and I do at times, but our Lord graciously lifted Sarah's eyes past her circumstances and toward his unfailing Word of promise.

This week, as you read about Sarah, remember this: the God who loved and brought Sarah through her doubt and failure is the same Jesus who calls you by name!

May your relationship with our risen Lord Jesus bring you much peace and joy as a woman of God!

By faith Abraham obeyed when he was called to go out to a place that he was to receive as an inheritance. And he went out, not knowing where he was going. Hebrews 11:8

Imagine a wife getting a call from her husband, telling her he's been named sole heir of a fabulous estate. They are to take possession immediately. He encourages her to start packing right away and advises her to take along a variety of clothing, since he's not sure what the weather will be like in their new location. In fact, he is not really sure where they are headed! If you were that wife, would the journey be a joy?

As Genesis 12 opens, Sarai and Abram set out on a lengthy trip. Neither of them knows for sure where they will end up. You may like surprises, but I check the Weather Channel two or three times just to make sure I pack the right clothes for a weekend getaway. Bear in mind that Abram was 75 years old and Sarai was 60 when they left home. I can't imagine where these two found their courage!

If we take a closer look, though, we see they relied on GPS—God's Promise of Salvation. God supplied the courage they needed time and time again through his good Word of promise. Every time the Lord speaks to one or both of them in Genesis, he adds more details to his promise. Eventually, the picture grows very clear. One of their descendants will be the Savior, first promised long centuries before in Eden's garden!

The Bible tells us one other important thing about this couple. Sarai was barren. Genesis 11:30 says it plainly: Sarai "had no child." Abram and Sarai continue childless year after year, chapter after chapter in Genesis. They lost hope more than once, but God reminded them over and over and over they could rely on his sure promises.

You can rely on God's promises, too, and especially on God's Plan of Salvation. In Jesus, you are God's beloved, forgiven child. A glorious inheritance awaits you, an inheritance Jesus won for you through his death on the cross.

All this is certain. Even so, your journey is bound to hold a few surprises. So don't forget to pack the promises!

Dear Jesus, fill me with the joy and peace that come from believing that you travel with me, today and forever . . .

By faith [Abram] went to live in the land of promise, as in a foreign land, living in tents with Isaac and Jacob, heirs with him of the same promise. For he was looking forward to the city that has foundations, whose designer and builder is God. Hebrews 11:9–10

Sarai was barren. For years she and Abram had waited and prayed for a child. In that culture, having many children was a symbol of the Lord's favor, while a closed womb was considered a punishment for one's sins. How devastated Sarai must have been as, month after month, she failed yet again to conceive.

But now God had promised a new land. The journey away from Haran would provide an escape from all the haughty and accusatory looks Sarai must have received in the marketplace. The move provided new hope, a fresh start for Sarai and Abram. God even gave them new names: Abraham, "father of many nations," and Sarah, "princess"!

Still, Sarah waited. She waited another 25 years! She went through menopause, maybe even holding her breath when decreasing hormone levels interrupted her monthly cycle. Still, no baby. Little by little, her joy seeped away.

What threatens to steal your joy? Do echoes from the past whisper your name? That hope dashed—again? and again and again? The lie you told that did irreparable damage? The worry that your kids will never heal from your divorce? The fear that abortion is an unforgivable sin? The angry words you spoke yesterday that are keeping you at arm's length from your husband or sister today?

God was faithful to the promises he made to Sarah, and he is faithful to the promises he has given to you, especially the precious promises of the forgiveness and healing won for you by Jesus through his death on the cross.

When you're tempted to look at your circumstances through the eyes of fear and doubt, when you're tempted to listen to lies that call you to account for past mistakes and failures, be encouraged by remembering who you are in Christ Jesus by his grace. Remember the new name God has given you: *Woman of God.* Remember the forgiveness he has given, forgiveness that frees you to live a life of joy.

Dear Jesus,
thank you for dying on the cross to take away all my sins. Help me to forgive myself and to live today joyfully in your love . . .

*By faith Sarah herself received power to conceive,
even when she was past the age, since she considered him
faithful who had promised. Hebrews 11:11*

*I*t was just an ordinary day. Perhaps Sarah had just lain down for an afternoon nap when Abraham burst into the tent, "Sarah, hurry! We have company! Make up some of those cakes! I need to go butcher a calf. Hurry!"

Cakes? Roast veal? It wasn't every day Sarah and Abraham entertained such distinguished guests. It's easy to understand why Sarah was eavesdropping at the back door of the tent, especially when she heard the visitors ask about her, by name!

But the prediction about her was laughable: "The LORD said, 'I will surely return to you about this time next year, and Sarah your wife shall have a son'" (Genesis 18:10).

Sarah tried to hide her lack of faith. She lied to God's face—denied having laughed at this, his promise. But God knew the truth about Sarah: her lies, her

unbelief, her jealousy, her rage and bitterness. God knew all about Sarah. But still, he loved her.

The Lord's response to Sarah's bitter rejection of his Word was simply to reaffirm his power and to restate his promise: "Is anything too hard for the LORD? At the appointed time I will return to you, about this time next year, and Sarah shall have a son" (Genesis 18:14).

Have you ever sneered at God? lied to his face? discounted his promises? relied too heavily on your own abilities? We may not live in tents, but women haven't changed much since Sarah's time. We still like the sound of our own name, hate to get caught doing wrong, and wish we could predict the future.

Sarah laughed again—a year later when Isaac was born, on schedule and as predicted, confirming the Lord's faithfulness.

As God came to Sarah in her doubts and fears, so he comes to us, reaffirming his power and restating his promises. Is anything too hard for the Lord? No. Did he send a Savior to die in your place, to rise again, and to defeat death for all time? Absolutely yes! Right on schedule and just as predicted. He will never leave you or forsake you. That's something to laugh in joy about!

Dear Lord Jesus, nothing is too difficult for you. Let your power and love open the floodgates of joy into my heart today . . .

Day 4
Faith that Persists

By faith Abraham, when he was tested, offered up Isaac, and he who had received the promises was in the act of offering up his only son, of whom it was said, "Through Isaac shall your offspring be named." He considered that God was able even to raise him from the dead, from which, figuratively speaking, he did receive him back. Hebrews 11:17–19

Sarah's story doesn't end in "happily ever after" with Isaac's birth. What must she have thought as Abraham left with young Isaac? They took along no animal for the sacrifice Abraham intended to offer. Had he shared God's instructions with Sarah? How would you react if your husband told you of a plan to sacrifice your only son, having been instructed by God to do just that?! (See Genesis 22:1–19.)

It's hard to understand Abraham's obedience. But Abraham obeyed. It's hard to believe he did that without Sarah's consent. Abraham's obedience and faith were almost certainly Sarah's, too.

For more than 100 years, Sarah had watched the Lord

working in her life, never failing to keep his promises. Could it be that Sarah, persistent in her faith, actually encouraged Abraham to trust God as he carried out this horrific assignment?

Hebrews 11 notes that Sarah considered God faithful to his promises. Perhaps God used her to encourage her husband to align his will with God's and then be ready to receive another miracle! We don't know for sure. We do know that Abraham and Isaac set out on a three-day journey into the wilderness. And we know that Abraham and Isaac both returned a week later. Sarah was surely overjoyed to see them. But surprised? I don't think so. She knew her Lord too well.

Like the ram God sent as a substitute for Isaac, Jesus Christ came as our substitute, the Lamb of God offered up for our sins in our place. Since God did that for us, we can trust him to keep all his other promises to us as well!

Let joy and confidence replace fear and doubt in your heart today because of what Jesus has done for you. Let confident joy in Jesus be the focus of your witness to God's unfailing love and faithfulness!

Dear Jesus, thank you for pursuing a relationship with me, and for the peace that comes from knowing you. When worry and fear threaten to steal my joy, remind me . . .

Day 5

Joy in the Journey
By Faith

My heart is glad . . . Psalm 16:9

Sarah's journey through life took place so long ago. How can it possibly hold any relevance for us today? Sarah knew nothing about Internet marketing, parent-teacher conferences, Zumba classes, or the latest posts on a friend's Facebook page. Sarah baked cakes on hot bricks, drew water from the wells in oases, and took trips on camels. What's more, God himself walked up to the front door of her tent and announced his unbelievable plan for her future!

Our lives are nothing like Sarah's! Still, in many ways, women really haven't changed that much over the years.

Genesis details many of Sarah's failures to trust the Lord's promises: her lies, her jealousies, her pride, and her seemingly relentless schemes to assert control over what was happening to her and her family. Over this past week, we have seen just a few examples.

Sarah was 127 years old when she died. She never met her daughter-in-law or spoiled her grandkids. Would Sarah understand our challenges? Would she recognize our feelings of disappointment? No doubt!

We may not bake cakes in an outdoor oven, but we recognize much from Sarah's life. Jealousy, doubt, and pride creep into our hearts at times, too. We appreciate her grief. She comprehends our disappointments. Human nature hasn't changed much, and neither have our Lord's gracious pardon, his support, and unfailing love.

The same God who was at work in the details of Sarah's life is involved in the details of your life, too. Nothing escapes his notice. Just as he enjoyed an intimate relationship with Sarah, so he wants that same kind of relationship with you. After all, he sent his own Son to Calvary's cross to make that possible!

Your Lord longs for you to know him as your faithful Promise Keeper, your source of forgiveness, peace, and joy, even in those situations that look impossible right now. He delights in keeping his promises to you—and he has made many of them!

Last, but not least, Sarah knew the joy of testifying to others of God's faithful love. So, too, your Lord wants you to know that joy—today and forever.

Listen! The encouragement of Sarah's life is unmistakable: let your heart be glad in the Lord!

Dear heavenly Father, you are the same, yesterday, today and forever. Let that truth fill me with joy and increase my trust and obedience to you . . .

Be Glad! Rejoice in God's Promises!

Just as God made and kept promises to Sarah, so he makes and keeps promises to you, woman of God! Here are just a few. Memorize one or all of them in the days ahead:

I am the good shepherd. I know my own and my own know me . . . I give them eternal life, and they will never perish, and no one will snatch them out of my hand. John 10:14, 28

I am the resurrection and the life. Whoever believes in me, though he die, yet shall he live, and everyone who lives and believes in me shall never die.
John 11:25–26

If we confess our sins, he is faithful and just to forgive us our sins and to cleanse us from all unrighteousness.
1 John 1:9

I will not leave you or forsake you.
Joshua 1:5

Whatever you ask in my name, this I will do. John 14:13

Ruth

A Joyful Journey of Selfless Service

The Book of Ruth takes us along on Ruth's life-changing journey. We watch as she endures the death of her husband; life in a strange, new land; and extreme poverty. We see her assume sole responsibility for her husband's mother. And we learn that the Lord is always, always a very present help in trouble (Psalm 46:1). Our Savior's faithful love never changes.

Ruth's life and ours differ in many ways. But no matter what circumstances we encounter in our own journey, we, too, can take joy and find peace in the God of Israel, "under whose wings [we] have come to take refuge!" (Ruth 2:12). May your relationship with our risen Lord Jesus bring you much peace and joy as a woman of God!

Elimelech, the husband of Naomi, died, and she was left with her two sons. These took Moabite wives; the name of the one was Orpah and the name of the other Ruth. They lived there about ten years, and both Mahlon and Chilion died, so that [Naomi] was left without her two sons and her husband. Ruth 1:3–5

Imagine it's Monday morning. Your alarm didn't go off. The kids have lost their homework. Traffic is backed up. You miss your first morning meeting. You're stuck in a downward spiral.

Every woman has times like these. Sometimes, things turn around within a few hours. Other times, the streak of negativity drags on for weeks or months or even years!

When we meet Ruth and Naomi in Ruth 1:1–14, both women are trapped in a spiral of negativity that has seemingly gone on forever. Their journey has taken them through famine and funerals into a life of poverty and chaos.

Naomi pleads with Ruth to escape further trouble by staying put in her homeland, Moab.

Ruth refuses. Instead, she clings to Naomi and, together, the two head back to Naomi's home in the land of Israel.

Looking at all this, we might say to ourselves, "Ruth must have been crazy! Why didn't she bail on Naomi and pursue a more promising future for herself?"

Why? Because Ruth had come to a living faith in Naomi's God! Ruth knew that her God-given place was with Naomi, no matter how difficult the journey ahead might prove. Ruth's life was hard, but she knew that Israel's God, Naomi's God, *her* God, was good.

Your good God is at work in your circumstances too. He is at work even when your life is a mess. He holds you in the very center of his heart, and he will unfailingly bring about his best for you. In the end, he provided everything Ruth could have dreamed—even an infant son and a place on the family tree of Jesus Christ himself!

How can you face your own downward spirals with joy? You are sure to have momentary doubts. But remember, your Lord's love is both personal and faithful. Jesus died for you on Calvary's cross! God gave his only Son into death for you. He gave you his best—he won't withhold the rest.

Lord Jesus, you are at work for my good through every circumstance of my life. Grant me peace as . . .

Ruth said, "Do not urge me to leave you or to return from following you. For where you go I will go, and where you lodge I will lodge. Your people shall be my people, and your God my God." Ruth 1:16

Selfishness sprouts early in life as children declare each toy "mine" and refuse to share. It grows even more dangerous as teens insist on what they want, when they want it, despite parents' warnings. Society reinforces it in adults as co-workers trample each other in pursuit of promotions, and friends betray each other to get ahead.

If you think that Ruth never struggled with selfishness, think again. For much of her life, Ruth worshiped the gods of Moab. Like most pagan deities, these gods promised worshipers prosperity, power, and control over their own destinies.

But the God of Israel changed Ruth's heart. At some point in the course of marrying Naomi's son and, then, mourning his death, Ruth came to faith in the true and living God. Ruth came to trust in the promised Savior. We hear Ruth affirm her faith in her assurance to Naomi, "Your God [will be] my God."

Ruth came to live in Israel, and the God of Israel came to live in Ruth. The Lord made it possible for her to follow Naomi in self-forgetful service.

Naomi desperately needed a friend, a sister in Christ. Ruth became that friend, that sister. In doing so, she gave up her family, friends, and the only home she had ever known. Ruth could do that because the infinite grace and mercy of Jesus had flooded her heart. Jesus made it possible for Ruth to serve Naomi in genuine joy.

All women have goals and dreams. There's nothing wrong with that, unless we put on blinders, choosing to ignore everything around us except our own selfish pursuits.

But even when we've done that—and we've all done that—we can turn to Jesus. We can confess our self-focus and ask our Savior for forgiveness. We can ask him to transform our self-serving hearts. And he will! In his cross we find the strength we need for self-forgetful service and the grace we need to love others with unselfish love.

Dear Savior,
it is all too easy to follow my own selfish path. Help me see the opportunities you give me to love others and then give me the strength to serve without hesitation . . .

[Naomi said,] "The man is a close relative of ours, one of our redeemers." Ruth 2:20

"I am woman; hear me roar!"

We love those lyrics, don't we? We are strong. We are invincible! We can do anything!! Until the challenges of real life intrude. Then, the promises of Helen Reddy's anthem quickly wear thin.

Does your car need $980 in repairs? Is your company downsizing? Do the angry words of a close friend sting? Have you begun to believe you've failed as a mom? At some points in life, all of us feel much more like a timid mouse than a roaring lion!

As Ruth and Naomi settled down in Bethlehem, the harsh reality of their situation became instantly clear. They were certainly independent, but not in a good way for women in that place, time, and culture. They had no one to protect or support them.

In a last-ditch effort to avoid starvation, Ruth volunteered to glean grain left in the fields after the harvesters had finished. It was hot, hard work. Backbreaking work.

Ruth had no way of knowing it as she labored, but help was on the way. That very day, the Lord would free Ruth and Naomi from all their fears and every uncertainty.

A wealthy landowner named Boaz owned the field where Ruth began her work. He immediately took notice of her. Quietly and in the background at first,

and then more openly in the days that followed, Boaz began to protect and provide for Ruth and Naomi.

Boaz had both the willingness and the legal standing to become a kinsman-redeemer for Ruth and Naomi. As a close relative, Boaz could lawfully reclaim Naomi's family property and rescue the widow and her daughter-in-law from poverty, danger, and shame.

Boaz pictures in a small and faint way all that Jesus would do for us in a glorious and powerful way. No matter how loudly we roar about our independence, no woman of God can safely journey through this life alone. We need the security of a kinsman-redeemer.

Jesus Christ is that Redeemer! He died for us on Calvary's cross and rose again, defeating death. In Jesus, we have the protection, provision, and security for which we long, the protection, provision, and security we need.

Lord Jesus, forgive me for thinking that I can do anything without you. Teach me to rely on your promises, even in the face of adversity . . .

Then the women said to Naomi, "Blessed be the LORD, who has not left you this day without a redeemer, and may his name be renowned in Israel!" Ruth 4:14

In March 1993, the "Storm of the Century" hit the eastern United States. At one point, the storm extended from the Gulf of Mexico into northern Maine and beyond. This region had seen plenty of blizzards before, but this one was different. It roared up the coast, dumping massive amounts of snow, with winds blowing at 70 miles per hour. When it finally blew itself out, nearly 300 people had died. It took $6 billion to repair the property damage left in its wake.

Living through a snowstorm like this is no easy task. Most people bring out the board games, watch reruns on television, or read a book. But as the winds continue to bluster, as we endure countless hours of house arrest, our spirits can easily start to droop. We get grumpy and short-tempered. We feel angry and powerless. Will it ever end?!

Naomi's life was much like that. She experienced a multitude of losses and hardships. Her spirit suffered and, eventually, she let people know it. When the townspeople of Bethlehem called her by her given name, Naomi, which means "pleasant," she fired back, insisting they call her Mara, meaning "bitter."

At times, Ruth must have thought about giving up on Naomi. Perhaps she bit her tongue to keep from shouting, "Snap out of it!" Maybe she was even tempted to walk away, to leave Naomi and her grief behind.

But that's not what happened. Ruth remained a faithful friend to Naomi. Her Christlike love and dedicated service brightened Naomi's life. Little by little, Ruth brought Naomi out of her bitterness. Little by little, God used Ruth to bring joy into Naomi's heart once again.

We all know people like Naomi. It's not easy to maintain a friendship with them. It can be even harder to share Jesus' love with them. But if we take a moment to see what lies behind their anger and hostility, we may be able to see them as Christ sees us—as sinners, dearly loved by God and redeemed by him. That perspective makes compassion and commitment possible.

Heavenly Father, keep me always mindful of those around me who need your peace and forgiveness. No matter their outward attitudes or actions, embolden me to show them your deep love . . .

Be glad in the LORD, and rejoice. Psalm 32:11

Do you remember floppy disks? There were billions of those plastic squares in use during the last two decades of the 20th century, but they didn't last. By the early 2000s, most computers were being made without floppy disk drives.

Technology had advanced, and most people treated their used floppy disks as trash. The disks were ugly and useless. Once we had harvested the data on them, what was the point of keeping them around?

British artist Nick Gentry has a different way of thinking about floppy disks. He has built his artistic career on "upcycling" obsolete technology. He takes what we see as useless garbage and turns it into stunningly beautiful artwork.

In much the same way, God "upcycled" Ruth. Think about her early life. Ruth knew nothing about the true God, his love, or his commands. She knew nothing of the promised Savior. She worshiped violent, vengeful idols, and had earned nothing from the Lord but his wrath. But the Lord God of Israel loved Ruth. Through an unlikely series of events, he brought Ruth to true faith. He turned Ruth's life into a work of art, into something stunningly beautiful! As the Lord worked

in her and through her, Ruth was able to show kindness, compassion, and loyalty in service to others. Forgiven in the Savior who was to come, Ruth was able to look past Naomi's bitterness. Confident in God's protecting love, Ruth could selflessly sacrifice her time and energies for others. Trusting in the coming Redeemer, Ruth could joyfully accept the loving protection of her earthly kinsman-redeemer, Boaz.

Like you and I, Ruth faced temptation all her life. Like us, she battled sin and knew how much she needed her Savior. Like us, Ruth knew that Savior's constant love, forgiveness, and acceptance.

Like Ruth, you and I have been upcycled. We have been cleansed and made new through Jesus' sacrifice on the cross. We have been blessed in unimaginably wonderful ways.

Now, he sends us in his name to share the blessings we have received. Ours is a joyful journey, marked by faith and Christlike service.

Dear Jesus,
my journey through life has
not been easy. When I feel like
I'm ready to quit, uplift me with your
grace and mercy. Flood my heart
with your joy and show me how to
share it with others . . .

A Lifelong Journey of Selfless Service

Ruth's journey through life took her from Moab to Bethlehem, from idolatry to true faith, from anonymity to a prominent place in the genealogy of Jesus. Where will your journey of joyful service take you?

Set aside a few moments to jot down some of the ways God has used you in the past. Don't limit yourself to the past few years. Think way back— even into childhood.

Now, analyze your opportunities for Christian service today. Note any foot-dragging or self-doubt you would like to change. Also note the people who could help you as you serve.

Next, brainstorm opportunities that lie open to you in the future. Don't stop with your service in the past and present. You have a lot of service left in you!

Finally, ask Jesus to guide you in saying yes to some things, no to others, as he leads and strengthens your love.

To many Christians, Deborah is a mere footnote in the history of God's people. Yet she has the singular honor of being the only woman appointed by God as both a judge and prophetess.

Deborah's responsibilities required faith and strength of character. At times she must have found her burdens quite daunting. But, like weary women of God who carry burdens today, she looked to the Lord for help. And he freely provided it!

God's power became Deborah's power. As you journey with her this week, may that same power rekindle your faith and turn responsibilities into privileges as your challenges blossom into joys.

Day 11

A Caring Heart:
You Are My Children

I, Deborah, arose as a mother in Israel. Judges 5:7

y son Mike shared the nuances of his baby James' only words in a Christmas letter: "Mama. Mama? Mama! MA-MA!" Translation: "I need you. Care for me. Help me! Right now!!" What depth of meaning one little word can carry!

Recognized in Israel as both a prophetess and judge, Deborah nonetheless chose to call herself "mother." Deborah's people, Israel, had lived under 20 years of foreign occupation. They had refused to repent, and the Lord had brought judgment for their sins.

Terrorized and threatened by Sisera, the head of King Jabin's Canaanite army, the spirit-wounded Israelites lived immobilized by fear. They needed to turn to their Lord in faith and rekindle their confidence in his love. They needed Mother Deborah.

What a job for that woman of God! Mothering one screaming toddler or stubborn teen exhausts any mom, yet Deborah joyfully took on an entire nation, especially their army. Where did she find the strength?

Deborah drew her power from the Lord. As he nourished her, she in turn could nurture Israel's ragtag army. The task of reviving the spirits of those once-bold men surely drained Deborah, but emboldened by God's love, she refused to give up.

As women of God, we, too, soak up God's love and pass it on to our "army"—our children, husband, friends, or the needy strangers we meet along life's way. Sometimes we stumble; often we tire. But still we forge ahead, knowing that Jesus forgives our sins. His Word of grace and hope revives us. We, in turn, forgive and rejuvenate others, sharing God's promised forgiveness and love.

How blessed we are to be women of God, infused with caring hearts and unlimited opportunities! Every tissue we offer to dry someone's tears, every empathic hug we give, marks a mothering moment. Best of all, we get to share a Savior who died and came to life again to bring peace and hope to each disheartened soul.

Impatience may sneak into our hearts when we give it our all, but fail to see results. Once I was leading a youth group made up of diverse individuals. A few of them were difficult, but one depressed, silent teen particularly challenged me. Years later, I received a note: "I know God brought you to me," it read. "You changed me, helped me, and listened to me." In his own time, God does bless the mothering we do in Christ's name.

Lord, show me how to be a mother with Deborah's heart. Help me . . .

March on, my soul, with might! Judges 5:21

I begged Mom to let me take my bike to the store. Reluctantly she agreed. Dangling a loaf of bread from the handlebars on the way home was a challenge—more of a challenge than I had anticipated! Suddenly, I plummeted into a hedge, tearing open the wrapper, spewing slices everywhere.

"Not so easy," Mom commented when she beheld my bedraggled half-loaf of salvaged bread.

Deborah's disheartened army felt the same about their odds of winning against General Sisera, the Canaanite. After all, Sisera's army boasted 900 iron chariots; Israel had none. Israel had few fighting men and even fewer weapons, while the Canaanite army had plenty of both. "Trust the Lord, and victory will be ours"? Easy for Deborah to say!

But Deborah knew a secret Israel's soldiers had forgotten: victory comes, not from weapons or mighty men of war, but from the Lord. We catch a glimpse of Deborah's confident joy in God as she marshals those bedraggled Israelite warriors to action. "March on with might!" she shouts, knowing the Lord marched with them.

I don't think Deborah's joy came easily. Challenges swamped her, as they do us when we care for rambunctious children, wipe down recurring spider webs, and tackle mountains of eternal laundry. And, mother or not, as women of God we regularly confront chronic illness, marital problems, aging parents, job loss, and life's frequent sorrows—endless struggles!

What do we do when stressors bombard? Deborah looked to her Lord. She couldn't change Israel's plight, but she could adjust their attitude. What God allows into our lives often can't be changed either, but as the Holy Spirit works in us, we *can* readjust our focus.

The Holy Spirit helps form our prayers. He teaches us to embrace each challenge as an opportunity to serve, and he infuses us with courage. Sometimes women of God fail; resentment elbows out our joy. But in Jesus' cross we receive unlimited forgiveness and new opportunities to try again.

Sometimes in our neediness we forget that the Lord doesn't expect us to carry heavy burdens alone. He provides agencies, caring people, and pastors to support us. He encourages prayer and promises to hear us.

Trials don't bypass believers. But Jesus, who suffered and died for us, invites us to rest in him. Then, even in the deepest valleys, we can rejoice!

Jesus, my burdens are often heavy. Help me to . . .

Now Deborah, a prophetess, the wife of Lappidoth, was judging Israel at that time. Judges 4:4

Bedtime, lunchtime, free time—time defines so many areas of our lives! The puzzle? Fitting all those "times" into twenty-four hours and finding quality "God-time."

No doubt, Deborah had time issues too. Married to Lappidoth, she wasn't just a prophetess and judge; she was also a wife and possibly a mother. Her name, Deborah, means "bee" and it hints at energy, hard work, and the desire to serve. Certainly Deborah possessed all three. But even the most industrious woman sometimes tires, and even Deborah couldn't call it a day when judging was finished. Lappidoth still needed dinner.

We, too, face time challenges. The modern age has given us laborsaving devices, but it hasn't managed to give us even one extra minute. We hold down a job—or two! We clean. We cook. We volunteer at church or at our children's school. Help! Where do women of God find time for joy given all the endless must-be-dones?

We find it in remembering that joy isn't a result of what we accomplish. It grows from remembering whose we are . . . the Lord's precious ones.

When we realize that all we do, we do for him, even mundane chores begin to feel less like drudgery and more like joy. Our busy lives are transformed by the privilege of serving him by serving those around us.

Imagine! The King of the universe invites us, his redeemed children, to converse with him. Even on whirlwind days, we can pray as we sit at our desk, mop a floor, or change a diaper.

But sometimes even our best intentions derail. We want to be women of God, but the treadmill just keeps churning. We fall exhausted into bed at night, God-time neglected. When we stumble across those ruts along our path, Jesus offers forgiveness in his cross. When our frustrations grow too great, our Lord offers to guide us as we look for ways to downsize commitments so we can give him top priority once more.

Is it possible to be busy as a bee and still have peace? Can joy grow in a garden of chaos for women of God? Yes! And, yes! God, the keeper of all good things, longs to fill us with his joy and peace. We need only ask!

It's hard to concentrate on my journey when I'm so busy, Lord. I need . . .

Deborah said to Barak, "Up! For this is the day in which the LORD has given Sisera into your hand. Does not the LORD go out before you?" Judges 4:14

When my son-in-law was learning to walk, he feared letting go of Mama's hand. Finally Mom gave him one end of a clothespin while she held the other end. When she quietly let go of the pin, Josh walked, on his own, not realizing his mother wasn't helping at all.

Deborah was Barak's clothespin. Finally ready to fight, the commander of Israel's army begged Deborah to accompany him into battle. She agreed. With an insight that must have come straight from the Holy Spirit, Deborah told Barak his hesitancy meant a woman would slay Sisera.

Later that day, just as Deborah had predicted, Jael drove a spike through Sisera's skull while he rested in her tent. Jael, not Barak, received all the credit for the enemy's untimely end.

Deborah's question in today's focus verse hints at her exasperation. Hadn't she mothered Barak? Hadn't she assured him of God's power? Hadn't she roused him to action? Again, she encourages him, "Does not the LORD go out before you?"

Like Deborah, mothers often encourage:

- "You can do it!"
- "Just try one bite!"

Mothers build up, shore up, and lift up their children. Trouble is, all that encouragement may leave a woman of God feeling empty. Who encourages the encourager?

As women of God, we know bottom-line that encouragement flows from the Lord. His courage at work in us gets us over the steep hills and through the frightening valleys in our journey through life. The Word proclaims Jesus' power to scale mountains, brighten lowlands, and defeat giants.

As women of God, we take this Scripture seriously: "Exhort one another every day" (Hebrews 3:13).

We "exhort" or "encourage" one another daily! It may be just a smile, a pat on the back, or a heartfelt thank you. While brief, all these encourage. A word of praise shared over coffee. A "hang-in-there" spoken to a struggling teen. These are encouragement blessings.

We might not help rout armies as Deborah did, but we *can* touch people, one smile at a time. And when we encourage others, the hope and joy we share boomerangs back to us, refreshing us for our own journey.

Dear Jesus, through the power of the Holy Spirit help me to encourage . . .

My heart is glad . . . Psalm 16:9

Many years ago my sister-in-law Ruth—a faithful Christian, mother, and kindergarten teacher—was killed in a car accident. At the funeral her pastor gave her a joyous commendation. He called her brief life "a song of praise."

Deborah's life was also a God-song. Read through Judges 5. What a beautiful, faith-filled chapter! As you read this song, look for Deborah's enthusiastic attitude of praise.

If you read carefully, you will notice something else, too. Deborah doesn't dwell on the part she played in Israel's defeat of the Canaanites. Rather, in godly humility, Deborah praises Barak, Jael, and the Israelite army. Most importantly, she thanks God for his deliverance over and over again.

As women of God, we have an even greater deliverance to celebrate. We stand in the shadow of our Savior's cross, delivered from death, and reveling in the eternal life our risen Lord has given us. We are completely forgiven and dearly loved by our heavenly Father. And the best is yet to come! We have every reason to be glad in the Lord. We have every reason to rejoice!

How we long to share that joy with those who travel with us through life! Sometimes, though, we find ourselves burned out, overcommitted, and facing challenges that smother our gladness.

We intend to encourage others but find ourselves ambushed by discouragement. Time pressures and the potholes along our path through life threaten to silence our song.

When we find ourselves in the shadows like that, our Lord calls us to drink deeply from his Word. He reminds us of his invitation: "Come to me, all who labor and are heavy laden, and I will give you rest" (Matthew 11:28).

In Jesus' healing rest, we gain strength to take up our cross, to journey onward, to share the Good News of salvation and peace with other weary travelers. In Jesus' healing rest, we find the courage to enter each new day with confident hope.

As we share our love for the Lord in word and action, our own lives are transformed. His grace at work in us makes our life-song bolder, our journey sweeter. And through the exquisite, inextinguishable joy our Savior gives, we—like Deborah and Ruth before us—become beautiful and humble songs of praise.

*My Savior,
I long to be a song of
praise. Show me . . .*

Busy as a Bee? Take Time for a Song of Joy!

As you journey through life, woman of God, what is most likely to sap your joy? Schedule overload? Stress? Discouragement? What makes that specific struggle so difficult?

Let us then with confidence draw near to the throne of grace, that we may receive mercy and find grace to help in time of need.
Hebrews 4:16

He is at my right hand, I shall not be shaken. Therefore my heart is glad, and my whole being rejoices.
Psalm 16:8–9

What would it mean for you to "approach [God's] throne with confidence"? What difference would it make if you were to "receive mercy" and "find grace"? How could it help your heart to be glad?

With these ideas in mind, find a piece of paper and write your own song or unrhymed poem of praise to God. It's okay to include challenges and failings, but remember to dovetail them into God's unfailing love and power.

Mary
A Joyful, Inspiring Journey

Mary, the mother of Jesus, is perhaps the most well-known woman of God in this devotional collection. Mary figures prominently in the New Testament Gospels. Most masters of the Renaissance did their best to capture her on canvas. Towns across the globe have been named in her honor—even Los Angeles, California.

This week we will explore Mary's journey of faith. Along the way there will be misunderstandings and moments of strength. There will be tears of joy and of sorrow. And in it all, we will see our Lord use Mary mightily to carry out his great plan of salvation.

Do not be afraid, Mary, for you have found favor with God. And behold, you will conceive in your womb and bear a son, and you shall call his name Jesus. Luke 1:30–31

WHAM! The deer ran out of the field and smack into the side of my car. I was shocked and shaken. Now I would have to call into work, notify the insurance company, arrange for repairs, and find alternate transportation. This was not what I had in mind for the day.

Have you ever had an experience that seemed to come straight out of left field and throw you for a loop? Perhaps it left you shaken and full of questions.

Mary, the mother of Jesus, had just such an experience. It flooded over her, triggering feelings of shock and confusion. Out of nowhere, the angel Gabriel appeared to Mary and announced that she would give birth to earth's long-awaited Messiah. God had broken into the life of this ordinary teenage girl. Now, she faced the challenge of a lifetime.

Mary responded to the announcement with a very logical question. "How will this be, since I am a virgin?" (verse 34). Mary wasn't being rude. She was pointing out, from a human perspective, the obvious flaw in the plan: she couldn't have a baby; she was a virgin. Patiently, the angel explained that Mary would conceive through the power of the Holy Spirit: "For nothing will be impossible with God" (verse 37).

Reassured, Mary believed God's promise and joyfully accepted the challenge.

Like Mary, you and I often have trouble understanding the ways of our Lord. We find ourselves tempted to point out what we see as the obvious flaws in what God asks of us. We insist we're not qualified. We explain that we are too busy, too frail, or too scared. We doubt God's promises and rebel against his will.

But our misgivings and outright rebellion cannot stop our Lord's love for us. Like Mary, we have found favor with God—in the life, death, and resurrection of the Son that Mary bore. We can confess our sins and find full forgiveness. In Jesus, the guilt of our rebellion has been wiped away. Our self-pity and false modesty have been drowned.

We can embark on any journey knowing that we are loved by God and fully equipped for the road ahead.

Dear Jesus,
teach me to step out in faith
and obedience as . . .

Mary treasured up all these things, pondering them in her heart. Luke 2:19

*I*t may be dark outside, but inside, the fluorescent lights glow and the checkout line winds to the back of the store. It's Black Friday and I've arrived early to take advantage of the Christmas sales. Now, however, my excitement has been replaced by impatience and irritation. I am tired. Children are wailing. How many coupons does that woman have?! Price check! Are you in line? Yes!

We all get stressed out. Christmas seems especially taxing, but it's not life's only stressful time. Throughout the year we find ourselves surrounded by noise, busyness—chaos! Exhausted, all we want is a moment's peace.

In this way, we have much in common with Mary as Luke 2 describes her. Heavily pregnant, she and Joseph have traveled a great distance. Arriving in Bethlehem, they are forced to lodge in a cave full of livestock. There, Mary gives birth. As she looks for a cradle for Baby Jesus, it soon dawns on her that she must turn an animals' feed trough into a cradle for the infant Son of God!

Then the riffraff show up. In that culture, shepherds stood on the lowest rung of the social ladder. They were considered as corrupt as tax collectors. Yet, there they stood, wanting to see and worship Jesus.

Who would have blamed Mary for demanding that everyone just get out and leave her and her little family alone? But Luke 2 records that instead Mary "treasured up all these things, pondering them in her heart" (verse 19).

Are you feeling overwhelmed today? exhausted? Is chaos too weak a word by half to capture it? In all you face, how can you hope to be as gracious as Mary? How could you ever hope to notice what God is doing, let alone treasure the moments and ponder them?

The answer is Jesus. Mary didn't just give birth to the Savior whom God had promised. She gave birth to the Prince of Peace. In the presence of our Lord who lived, died, and rose again for us, we can have peace. We need not worry or stress. We can joyfully claim our royal title. We are women of God, daughters of the King, cherished by the one who will forever be our peace.

Dear Jesus,
you are my peace as
I journey step by step through
life. Help me remember that,
especially when . . .

After three days they found [Jesus] in the temple, sitting among the teachers, listening to them and asking them questions. Luke 2:46

An old story tells of a tourist in New York City who asked directions of a man carrying a violin case: "How do you get to Carnegie Hall?" The violinist replied, "Practice."

The thought "practice makes perfect" is not new. In fact, Mary and Joseph spent their entire lives striving to do the right thing, practicing the Law of Moses, detail by detail.

Luke 2 tells us that they presented Jesus in the temple according to that Law. Later in that same chapter, they travel to Jerusalem with 12-year-old Jesus to celebrate Passover. Again, according to the Law.

But on their way home, Mary and Joseph notice that Jesus is not with them. Momentary worry quickly balloons into a frantic search. When they finally locate him—teaching in the Temple—Mary gives him a talking-to. "Why have you treated us so?" she asks (verse 48). Gently, Jesus asks, "Did you not know that I must be in my Father's house?" (verse 49).

Imagine Mary's confusion. Whatever could Jesus mean? Just this: Jesus knew and was living out his larger purpose. His parents obeyed the Law. Pious and well-intentioned though they were, their obedience was only partial, imperfect. Jesus had come to fulfill the Law for them and for us, to fulfill it completely.

At times on our journey through life we may feel like Mary. We have tried to do the right things. And yet, we are caught off-guard when life doesn't go our way. Like Mary, we ask God, "Why have you treated us so?"

Jesus fulfilled the Law for us, obeying it perfectly. Then he died and rose again to remove the penalty of our sin forever. The plan to win eternal salvation has been in God's heart forever. You and I have a part in bringing the Good News of it to others. Anything that happens to us can open the door to new opportunities for witness.

We don't always understand life's zigs and zags, but we can lean on the promises of our God whose love for us never, ever changes. We can't know what our future holds, but we do know the one who holds that future—and us—in his nail-scarred hands!

Lord Jesus, sometimes I forget that you have given me a part in your eternal purposes. Remind me . . .

When the wine ran out, the mother of Jesus said to him, "They have no wine." And Jesus said to her, "Woman, what does this have to do with me? My hour has not yet come." His mother said to the servants, "Do whatever he tells you." John 2:3–5

Have you ever received something unexpected? Perhaps someone sent you flowers for no reason or you received a birthday card from an old friend. Maybe a co-worker brought donuts for the Monday meeting. Isn't it nice to be pleasantly surprised?

John 2 starts with an unpleasant surprise. Jesus, some of his disciples, and Mary are all attending the same wedding feast, and the wine has run out. Wedding celebrations at the time lasted many days and often the whole town showed up. Running out of anything was not only a problem, it was a disgrace to the hosts.

Mary spots the problem and tells Jesus. She then instructs the servants to do whatever Jesus tells them. Jesus has the servants fill six large containers with water and when they have done so, to take a cup to the master of the feast.

Everyone in attendance that day soon knew that Jesus had created more than 120 gallons of the finest wine

imaginable! Not only
had Jesus provided
for this young couple
in a time of need,
he had done far, far
more than they could
have ever expected!

Jesus is our provider, too. Yet how quick
we are to point out the problems in our lives. We rush to
identify crises and drama in the lives of those we love.
We panic. We forget we can trust God to provide for us.
We scheme and scurry to provide for ourselves.

Jesus is our provider. He gives all we need for this life,
but he doesn't stop there. Jesus has provided abundantly
for our spiritual needs, too. When sin separated us from
our heavenly Father, Jesus came to earth to restore that
relationship. In the perfect life, death, and resurrection of
Christ, our sins are forgiven. By faith in him, we become
heirs of heaven, daughters of heaven's High King.

Jesus is our provider. And he is never stingy! Whether
we need daily bread or pardon for our many sins, Jesus
will not let us down. We are
loved and cared for
throughout our
earthly journey
and on into
eternity.
What joy!

Dear Jesus,
forgive me when I
fail to trust in you.
Teach me . . .

Therefore my heart is glad . . . Psalm 16:9

As we come to the end of the week, we also come to the last passage in Scripture to mention Mary. Throughout this week, we have seen the Virgin set out on her journey through life as the mother of the Savior. Humility. Gentleness. These were her hallmarks.

We saw Mary sit peaceful in the presence of the Infant Jesus, surrounded by lowlifes and livestock on that first Christmas night. We watched Mary dutifully raise the Boy Jesus in accordance with the Law of Moses—the Law he had come to fulfill. We rejoiced with Mary as she witnessed Jesus' abundant provision at Cana's wedding feast.

We see her again now in Acts 1, and much has happened since that day in Cana! "All these with one accord were devoting themselves to prayer, together with the women and Mary the mother of Jesus, and his brothers" (verse 14).

Mary has seen her son, God's Son, heal the sick, cast out demons, and forgive sins. She has endured his arrest and torture. She has stood, grieving, at the foot of the cross while her son takes his last, labored breaths.

So imagine Mary's surprise on Easter morning. Imagine her, still grieving, sleep-deprived, in John's home (John 19:27), surrounded by a new family. Imagine the knock at the door as someone arrives with news, news almost too good to be true: Christ is risen!

Christ is risen indeed! Too often, though, we live as people of death. We doubt. We grieve our circumstances. We work hard to please God, but fail to keep his commandments and mourn our own frail and fleeting willpower.

This is not God's intention! In Jesus, we are free to be women of God, women of joy and eternal life. We cannot earn God's forgiveness. Jesus earned it for us. He didn't stay nailed to the cross, our sins heaped upon him. He rose from death! He is our living Savior, the one who brings us life!

Acts 1 reveals that after the Resurrection, Mary lived out her life as one of Jesus' disciples—a life of worship, fellowship, and prayer. That's our new life, too. In Jesus' name, we are free to serve, to pray, to enjoy life in the family of God.

Precious Savior, thank you for living, dying, and rising for me. Today I especially praise you for . . .

As daughters of the risen King, we are forgiven and free to live lives of prayer, worship, and joy in the family of God—just like Mary.

Take a walk today as you pray for someone . . .

※ facing a great challenge who needs encouragement;

※ who needs to know the peace of Jesus;

※ struggling with the free grace and the undeserved love of Jesus; or

※ who needs to know Easter joy and walk in it.

When you return from your walk choose at least one of the people for whom you prayed and contact them via note, e-mail, or text message. Remind them of Jesus' love. Tell them you have prayed for them. Assure them that our Lord is always ready and willing to hear and answer their prayers, too.

"What a temper!" If that were how you'd describe Martha, you'd be right—but only in part. Martha's angry outburst about an unfair division of labor the day Jesus came to visit (Martha=everything; Mary=nothing) makes her . . . what? A normal, authentic woman!

If your responsibilities sometimes overwhelm you, you can relate to Martha. If you want everything to be just right for your guests, you can understand Martha. If you have ever hoped to be remembered for the times you help and heal, learn and love, listen and lean on Jesus, then you'll want to get to know Martha.

Get to know her as someone just like you—a woman of God whom Jesus loves.

[Martha] said to him, "Yes, Lord; I believe that you are the Christ, the Son of God, who is coming into the world." John 11:27

$\mathcal{B}$reaking news:

⁂ "Wedding Guest Takes Water, Makes Wine!"
⁂ "Nazarene Feeds 5,000 with Few Fish!"
⁂ "Preacher Sends Lame Man Leaping!"

Everyone had heard, including Martha of Bethany. For Martha, however, these events held special significance. The man everyone was talking about was family friend and frequent houseguest, Jesus.

Martha knew Jesus as someone who enjoyed lively conversation, who stopped by her house for needed food and rest. But she also recognized him as God's long-promised One. She listened to his teachings, pondered his parables, and saw that his powers matched the prophets' predictions of what the Messiah would do. Martha was a woman of God, a woman of faith.

Martha also was a woman who experienced life's ups and downs. One of those downs came when her brother, Lazarus, fell ill. Since Jesus was nearby, Martha sent word, asking him to come quickly. Surely he would want to heal Lazarus, his close friend. Everyone knew Jesus' power over sickness. Yet Jesus didn't come, and furthermore, offered no reason why he couldn't—or wouldn't—help.

The sting of this rejection surely intensified Martha's sorrow. Four days later, when he finally did arrive, Martha could barely control her anger and disappointment. It was then that Jesus showered her with divine grace, reminding her that he was the Resurrection and the Life. It was then that Jesus did what Martha thought lay beyond even his power—he called Lazarus from the grave!

Now Martha recognized Jesus' identity even more fully. Now she believed in a much deeper way his personal care for her. Now she received from him far more than she expected—her brother's life!

You have heard about Jesus' miracles and ministry, his death and resurrection. Now let him take you on a journey to an even higher—even more enlightened—faith! What burdens your heart today? Talk to him about it, and then remain teachable as he deepens your trust in him. Be patient, for he will act. Stay faithful, for he delights in showering you with his grace.

Expect that your joy will be full, because your Lord, your Friend, blesses in surprising, "breaking-news" ways!

Lord Jesus,
your cross proves your love
and power in ways much deeper
than I understand, than
I can understand!
Help me . . .

Martha was distracted with much serving. Luke 10:40

Perhaps it was when her parents died that Martha took charge of the household. She made a comfortable home for her siblings, Mary and Lazarus. But her duties went far beyond that. As head of a prominent family in Bethany, Martha was expected to offer hospitality to travelers, provide for the needs of the poor, and live an exemplary life. She met her responsibilities with energy and intelligence.

Martha served admirably. But how her mind reeled when the daily to-dos piled up, sudden emergencies shattered her plans, and unexpected guests vied for her attention. You know how it feels when the day is done, but you aren't! Busy Martha was so focused on serving others that she occasionally lost sight of what she herself needed: spiritual sustenance.

Jesus couldn't help but notice. During one of his visits, Martha rushed frantically to spread a picture-perfect meal before him, while Mary sat serenely at his feet. If you had been Martha, what would you have said? Martha said it, and in no uncertain terms. "She went up to him and said, 'Lord, do you not care that my sister has left me to serve alone? Tell her then to help me'" (Luke 10:40).

"Martha, Martha!" With a gentle rebuke and grace-filled smile, Jesus prompted her to rethink her priorities. Her service was important, but without the nourishment Jesus could offer, it became an all-encompassing burden. "Let *me* serve *you*, Martha!" his tone of voice pleaded as he tenderly led her from frantic action to quiet repose, calling her attention to what is eternal.

The Word of God was for Martha—and is for you—spiritual sustenance. It's the reason for joy in all you do, and it will be your source of joy for all eternity.

Jesus showed Martha that she was more than the sum of her service. Her spiritual experience mattered! His words pointed out that sometimes the most accomplished among us can learn something from those whose gifts are less obvious or less celebrated.

Just as he did for Martha, Jesus wants to take you on a journey from stress to stillness, from panic to peace of mind. He invites you to put him first, and then take on your responsibilities. He wants you to value yourself by letting him nourish you with his love.

He opens you to allow the gifts of others to bless your life, as your gifts bless theirs. Jesus welcomes you into the peace of his presence.

*My Savior,
your gifts sound too good
to be true!
Forgive me for . . .*

"Lord, do you not care that my sister has left me to serve alone?" Luke 10:40

Martha hid nothing from Jesus. In this case, she complained to him about her sister, Mary. Couldn't he see that Mary wasn't pulling her weight in the kitchen?

In the incident we read about a few days ago, Martha also complained to Jesus about his actions! Didn't he realize that his delay in coming to heal Lazarus led to her brother's death? Her voice may have had something of an edge, too, when she informed Jesus that Lazarus' four-day-old tomb would reek of death. Didn't he know?

Subjected to Martha's ill temper, most of us would respond in kind. Certainly we'd want to take her down a peg or two! But not Jesus.

Instead, he responded with grace. Far from scolding her for complaining about her sister, he gently invited her to relax. Far from resenting her for questioning his judgment, he kindly walked beside her in her sorrow. Far from scorning her limited knowledge and faith, he forgave and quietly challenged her to watch—just watch!

You know what happens! Jesus understood, he cared—he wept!—and then he raised Lazarus from the grave. How it all must have come together for Martha! Her outbursts

of irritation and Jesus' compassionate responses proved that she need never play-act in front of him. Though Jesus was her Savior and Redeemer, he required no show of slavish deference, fake happiness, or false piety. Why? Because he was also her Savior and Friend; she could speak to him honestly, friend to Friend.

Your journey with Jesus is a journey to becoming more fully you—authentically you. You can tell it like it is, even when it isn't pretty. If someone else is the problem, tell Jesus; and if he is the problem, tell him that, too. If you know the facts, or think you do, tell him. Be honest, because there's nothing you can hide from him—he's your Lord. There's no part that he wants you to hide from him—he's your Friend.

The compassion, kindness, and forgiveness Jesus showed to Martha in her anger and stubbornness is the same compassion, kindness, and understanding he extends to you. Jesus is your Friend. He will never leave you. Let him lead you to your joy!

Jesus, you are my Friend! That truth overwhelms me with joy. Teach me to be honest . . .

A woman named Martha welcomed [Jesus] into her house. Luke 10:38

artha had choices. She belonged to a comfortable, probably affluent, household. In the small town of Bethany, her family may have been the most prominent and influential one.

Certainly Martha could have distanced herself from less fortunate families by pursuing pleasure and enjoying leisure. Yet that's not what she chose. With her time and her resources, Martha practiced what Jesus preached: to whom much is given, much is required (Luke 12:48).

Picture Jesus and one, two, or three disciples entering Martha's well-appointed home. Here she offered them a place to rest after weeks of walking the dusty paths of Galilee and Judea. With Martha, Mary, and Lazarus, they could relax in pleasant surroundings, savor well-prepared meals, and share conversation with close friends.

Jesus graciously received Martha's generosity, but at the same time, he was blessing her more generously than she could ever have imagined. While she served food for the body, Jesus was serving far more—food for the soul. As she offered the gift of friendship, he was offering far more—the friendship of God. While she gave of her time, energy, skills, and resources, he was giving far more—his life, so Martha could know the joy of relationship with him forever.

Martha's work, motivated by the Holy Spirit, received Jesus' approval and support. In his approval and support, she found Spirit-given strength and vitality for even further service. And in this further service, she was able to recognize herself clearly as the heart and hands of God among his people.

You, too, have been given much, and you have choices. How are you using your time, energy, abilities, skills, and resources? Are you doing what you can to make life more pleasant for others? How can you give of yourself in even deeper, more meaningful ways than you are now?

Your Spirit-empowered generosity to others is food for your soul, for it increases your faith in Jesus' ability to meet your own needs. Your Spirit-enabled giving to "the least of these" is friendship with him, for it assures you that you are walking with him in your everyday life. Your Spirit-enlivened heart and hands are his heart and hands, serving with joy every step of the journey, for he first served you.

*Dear Jesus,
you loved and you gave.
You gave your life for me on
the cross! Forgive my frequent
bouts of self-centeredness.
Then show me . . .*

Therefore my heart is glad . . . Psalm 16:9

Without a doubt, Martha was a woman of God. Through the work of the Holy Spirit, she recognized in Jesus God's long-promised Messiah, and she had faith in him. She cared for others, blessing her family, friends, and community with her love and service. But was she perfect? Far from it!

Busy and purposeful, Martha became irritable when things weren't getting done the way she thought they should. Outgoing and energetic, she criticized those whose personality, priorities, and energy levels did not match her own. Accustomed to taking charge, she chided Jesus for his apparent negligence when she needed him most. If Jesus had sat her down, wagged his finger in her face, and delivered a harsh lecture, no one would have been surprised!

But he didn't. Jesus responded with grace. In Martha's ill temper, Jesus saw her need for rest, so he reminded her that there is rest in him. In her criticism of others, Jesus revealed his love not just for Martha, but for Mary and Lazarus, too—different temperaments, gifts, abilities, and talents, but the same infinite love. In Martha's need to control, Jesus demonstrated his better control by working things out for her present good and ultimate joy.

Think about it! In her exhaustion, Martha experienced Jesus' rest. In her weakness, she knew his forgiveness. In her grief and confusion, she recognized his power and authority over all sorrows, even death. Jesus embraced Martha, imperfections and all. He did not reject her. Rather, he continued to lead her on her journey to joyous living. Why? "Jesus loved Martha and her sister and Lazarus" (John 11:5).

Our own journey to joyous living starts in that same place—our Lord's infinite love. You and I are "imperfect," too. We get tired, grumpy, and angry. We have regrets, make mistakes, and often veer off in the wrong directions.

Despite it all, Jesus responds to us with grace! Enter his rest; even a few minutes of solitude with him will replenish your heart and soul. Accept his forgiveness; lay your shortcomings at his feet, and leave them there. Value your gifts; whatever they may be, Jesus prizes them far more than you know. And most of all, love yourself, because your Friend, Lord, and Savior loves you. Woman of God, let your heart be glad in him!

My Friend, how I need your love . . .

Woman of God, You Can't Do It All!

As you conclude this week's devotions, spend
some time in reflection, journaling, and prayer.
Consider questions like these:

What do I most admire about Martha?

When am I most like her?

**In what ways is my relationship
with Jesus like hers and how is
it different from hers?**

*Would I like to change any of my
answers to any of these questions?*

What will I say to Jesus about that?

Woman of God
Joy in the Journey

Sarah—desert sand between her toes,
and joyful in the journey . . .

Ruth—selfless as she served,
and joyful in the journey . . .

Deborah—the courageous warrior,
and joyful in the journey . . .

Mary—humble in God's chosen path,
and joyful in the journey . . .

Martha—friend of Jesus,
and joyful in the journey.

My sisters, faithful in Christ.
For now. Forever!

If this book has made a difference in your life or if you have simply enjoyed it, we would like to hear from you. Your words will encourage us! If you have suggestions for us to consider as we create books like this in the future, please send those, too.

❀ **Send e-mail** to editor@CTAinc.com and include the subject line: WOG5SC

❀ **Write to**
Editorial Coordinator,
Department WOG5SC, CTA, Inc.
PO Box 1205, Fenton, MO 63026-1205

❀ **Or leave a comment at** share.CTAinc.com